real

GUIDE TO

YOUR FIRST JOB

MEAGAN HASSELL

Real U Guides

Publisher and CEO:
Steve Schultz

Editor-in-Chief:
Megan Stine

Art Director:
C.C. Krohne

Graphic Designer:
Diane Smith

Illustration:
Mike Strong

Production Manager:
Alice Todd

Editorial Assistants:
Cody O. Stine
Gabriel A. Wildau

Library of Congress Control Number: 2004090908

ISBN: 0-9744159-7-9

First Edition
10 9 8 7 6 5 4 3 2 1

Copyright ©2004
Real U, Inc.

Published by
Real U, Inc.
2582 Centerville Rosebud Rd.
Loganville, GA 30052

www.realuguides.com

Real U is a trademark of Real U, Inc.

Photo Credits:

Cover and Page 1: Photodisc Collection/Getty Images; Page 3: Jean Louis Batt/Getty Images; Page 4: Photodisc Collection/Getty Images; Page 5: Pen, Photodisc Collection/Getty Images; Striding girl on cell phone, John Kelly/Getty Images; Girl in pink, Daly and Newton/Getty Images; Man with laptop, Chad Baker/Ryan McVay/Getty Images; Jackets on hangers, Steve Cole/Getty Images; Page 7: Andersen Ross/Getty Images; Page 8: Waiter pouring wine, Steve Mason/Getty Images; Pocket watch, Photodisc Collection/Getty Images; Page 10: John Kelly/Getty Images; Page 12: Digital Vision/Getty Images; Page 13: Bryan Mullenix/Getty Images; Page 14: Legs walking, Digital Vision/Getty Images; Pen, Photodisc Collection/Getty Images; Page 15: Andy Sotiriou/Getty Images; Page 16: Manchan/Getty Images; Page 17: Two guys talking, Colin Hawkins/Getty Images; Three people, Manchan/Getty Images; Page 18: Chad Baker/Ryan McVay/Getty Images; Page 19: ArtToday; Page 20: Sandy islands with trees, Photodisc Collection/Getty Images; Page 21: Waiting room, Holos/Getty Images; Page 22: Telephone, Photodisc Collection/Getty Images; Woman with pad and laptop, Photodisc Collection/Getty Images; Page 23: Digital Vision/Getty Images; Page 24: Digital Vision/Getty Images; Page 25: Woman with flowers, Manchan/Getty Images; Workman with equipment, Phil Boorman/Getty Images; Woman in headset, ArtToday; Page 26: Photodisc Collection/Getty Images; Page 27: Photodisc Collection/Getty Images; Page 28: RubberBall Productions/Getty Images; Page 30: Bryan Mullenix/Getty Images; Page 32: Digital Vision/Getty Images; Page 33: Chef, Manchan/Getty Images; Rock climber, RubberBall Productions/Getty Images; Swimmer, Andersen Ross/Getty Images; Page 36: Photodisc Collection/Getty Images; Page 40: Daly and Newton/Getty Images; Page 42: Digital Vision/Getty Images; Page 43: Janis Christie/Getty Images; Page 44: Steve Cole/Getty Images; Page 45: Woman in red sweater, Mark Scott/Getty Images; Man tying tie, Andersen Ross/Getty Images; Construction worker, Photodisc Collection/Getty Images; Page 47: Group at computer, Jim Arbogast/Getty Imaages; Mountain biker, Photodisc Collection/Getty Images; Page 48: Plush Studios/Getty Images; Page 50: Photomondo/Getty Images; Page 52: ArtToday; Page 54: Photodisc Collection/Getty Images; Page 55: Manchan/Getty Images; Page 57: Manchan/Getty Images; Page 58: John Lamb/Getty Images; Page 60: Digital Vision/Getty Images; Page 61: Jim Arbogast/Getty Images; Page 63: Rubberball Productions/Getty Images.

real U

GUIDE TO
YOUR FIRST JOB

MEAGAN HASSELL

You Need a Real Job...

You're out in the real world now, right? Maybe your parents told you to get a job or get out. (Could be worse—they could have told you to get a job and get out.) Or maybe you just finished college, and you're wondering what you can possibly do with a degree in sociology. (Our recommendation: frame it.) Or perhaps you're still in high school and you're looking for a part-time job so that when you and your friends hit the movies, you won't have to sneak in the back door.

Any way you slice it, job hunting can be a little tricky—and a little terrifying—at any stage of your life, no matter how qualified you are. But it can also be the most excitement you've had since you hot-wired the elevator at your old school.

So, don't panic. We've got all the tips you need for finding the right job, applying, writing a résumé, interviewing, and even leaving your first job when you realize what you're really worth—plus everything in between. So turn the page and get ready to get off your parents' couch.

And Welcome to **real U**

4

GUIDE TO
YOUR FIRST JOB
TABLE OF CONTENTS

QUIZ ARE YOU

Some people have "Hire me!" written in big letters all over them, and—big surprise—these are the guys who always end up with the good jobs. On the other hand, some people have "Hire me!" written in big letters all over their nice new suits—and all they wind up with are monster dry cleaning bills. Take this quiz to find out whether you've got a knack for getting hired, or whether you're going to need a really good stain remover.

1.

Let's say you've landed yourself a prime job interview at a major corporation. You're going to think very carefully about what to wear to the interview because...

A. If you can find the right outfit, you're sure every member of the opposite sex will be swooning all over the conference tables.

B. It's important that your future employers understand your personal sense of style—you don't want them to think you'll cover up your tats just to please the Man.

C. You want your interviewer to know that you can dress appropriately for the work environment.

EMPLOYABLE?

2.

Somehow you manage to get hired by a local party planning service as a client coordinator. Your first big task is setting up a meeting with a potential new client. For some reason, your boss won't listen to your ideas about using an orange-and-fuchsia color scheme for the table settings. Your solution?

A. Laughter is the best medicine, so you make jokes at the boss's expense and mumble sarcastic comments about his taste in table linens under your breath.

B. Having a job is nice, but if this guy doesn't understand the beauty of fuchsia, you're going to buy a Winnebago and head for Taos.

C. You figure you can make a big impression once you've earned some trust. For now, you're happy to take orders and let the personal stuff slide.

more quiz

3.

After the party planning disaster, you land a job waiting tables. The customers seem to like your big personality, but the manager is getting on your back about your wine selling skills. You:

A. Smile demurely and avoid the question by telling the manager you like his or her shirt. Try to seal the deal by batting your eyelashes when you ask if he or she has been working out.

B. Give him what you've been giving your customers—a whole lot of personality and a sassy attitude.

C. Admit that you've been slacking on alcohol sales, and ask if the manager can give you any pointers that might help.

4.

Your idea of "on time" is:

A. It depends on who's managing—some of the managers give you 10 minutes leeway, while others won't even notice if you're an hour late.

B. As soon as "Take My Breath Away" stops playing on your car radio.

C. Whatever your boss says it should be—or, actually, you plan to arrive twenty minutes earlier, just in case there's an overturned poultry truck on the interstate that could make you late for work.

5.

One of your co-workers is getting on your nerves, and the conflict is starting to distract you from your work. What's the solution?

A. Tell your boss that the co-worker has been stealing and get him booted out of there.

B. Conflict doesn't belong in the work place—ask the sucker if he wants to take it outside.

C. Try to resolve things diplomatically. If that fails, distance yourself from the problem. Finally, ask your boss for help resolving the conflict.

SCORING

This quiz was supposed to be a no-brainer, but in case you need it spelled out for you, the right answers are C. Give yourself one point for each right answer.

4-5 points: Congratulations. You don't need to write "Hire me!" on your clothes, because you've already got it stamped on your forehead—in the form of good employee instincts. With a little advice, you'll be a shoo-in.

2-3 points: You could probably use some help brushing up on your professional skills. It's not the end of the world. Read on and you'll learn everything you need to know to get your shoe in the door.

0-1 point: Oh, dear. Looks like you're more likely to put your shoe in your mouth (along with your foot) than get it in the door at your first job. But hey, at least you had the good sense to check out this book. Keep reading—unless you like the taste of shoe leather.

JOB HUNTING
STEP BY STEP

O.K., we admit it. There's a lot about job hunting that's even less fun than watching a _Partridge Family_ marathon on TV. It's a process that combines a boatload of rejection with a punishing dollop of humiliation. Who really enjoys asking friends, relatives, and acquaintances for big favors, for instance? Or summarizing your entire life history on a single sheet of paper?

Yeah, some aspects of job hunting are pretty much on the bottom of that list of Things You Want To Do Before You're Dead. But some aspects—like finding out what you want to do with your life, or learning how to talk about your best qualities—are at the top of that list, or somewhere near the top, or at least they should be. And unless your plans for the future involve traveling the world on your multi-million dollar trust fund, bilking little old ladies out of their life savings, or selling your plasma for cash, you'll probably need to get a job someday soon.

The good news is that it doesn't matter whether you're a high school student, a college grad, or a thirty-something mooch who has run out of friends' couches to sleep on—the job hunting skills you need are all pretty much the same. Sure, you may not need a résumé and cover letter to get a job in a burger joint (although it's not going to hurt). But the basics—tracking down jobs, networking, applying, and interviewing—stay the same.

So get ready—and get psyched!—for the first step in the process. After all, finding a job to apply for is more than half the battle. No one's going to be impressed by your great interviewing skills if all you do is practice them on your cat!

There are four tried and true ways to find job openings. Not necessarily in the order of their effectiveness, they are:

1. **Read the newspaper classified ads.**
2. **Hit the streets to call on potential employers in person.**
3. **Network with family, friends, and acquaintances.**
4. **Do an online job search.**

In general, you'll be more successful finding a good job if you use more than one tactic at once. But the time-honored tradition of circling want ads in red lipstick is an excellent way to start. (If you don't have any red lipstick, mauve or some other subdued color will do.)

GET YOUR HANDS DIRTY: SCOURING THE CLASSIFIEDS

Obviously you'll be starting with the want ads in your local paper, but check out the other sections of the paper, too. Business, technology, and education sections often have business technology, and educational job listings (no surprise).

The most important thing to remember when applying for jobs through the classifieds is that time is of the essence. Competition is fierce, so don't peruse the paper on Sunday, casually send out your

application on Thursday, and expect a call. Be ready to send out your cover letter and résumé immediately—everyone else is. "What cover letter and résumé?" you ask? Check out How to Write a Great Résumé on Page 27, and How to Write a Great Cover Letter on Page 37.

If Monday rolls by and you still haven't spotted a single job you want to apply for, move on to some other publications. If your city has a free weekly paper, check out its listings. Although there usually won't be as many ads in these free rags, they're also read by fewer people, so you stand a better chance of getting hired.

Large national companies—like, say, Coca-Cola or the CIA—often advertise in large national newspapers. If you're willing to relocate for a really good job, check out the *New York Times*, *Wall Street Journal*, or the *Washington Post*.

If you're interested in a very specific job, like cattle ranching or back-hoeing, hit the library and check out trade publications— magazines or journals that focus on a specific businesses or industries.

Finally, make sure to look at the newspaper classifieds online. They're often posted earlier than print ads, so you can get the jump on all the other job seekers.

DECODING THE ADS

Classified ads could be written in standard English, but that would be too easy! Instead, they're written using a complicated code that only insiders understand, with phrases like "fast-paced environment," and "self-starter," which seem meaningful but can be baffling. Before you start sending in cereal box tops for a top secret Job Seekers Decoder Ring, check out our handy key to the classified ads, decoded.

FAST-PACED ENVIRONMENT:
Unless the ad is for a position training race-horses, this means the job is deadline-driven and often stressful.

SELF-STARTER:
The company wants you to be able to fill your day productively—presumably they've got better things to do than baby-sit, (although they might just be lazy, and want you to do all the work).

WILLING:
You will do what you're told and like it.

OPEN AVAILABILITY:
Be ready to work hideous hours.

CHEERFUL:
The person who previously held this position had the personality—and possibly the wardrobe—of an executioner. Smile please.

CLASSIFIED ADS COULD BE WRITTEN IN STANDARD ENGLISH, BUT THAT WOULD BE TOO EASY!

EOE:
Equal Opportunity Employer. Businesses are required by law to hire without regard to race, creed, color, ethnicity, etc. When businesses list "EOE" in their ads, they're just pointing out that they know the law and obey it.

13

Beating the streets

GET YOUR SHOES DIRTY: BEATING THE STREETS

Beating the streets is probably the simplest form of job hunting there is: you go door to door with your résumé in hand and hope to find a manager in a good mood. The "beating the streets" part comes when you get turned down so many times that you feel the need to beat your head against the pavement in frustration. Before you do that, check out our tips on how to sell yourself door-to-door. These generally work best if you're looking for a position in the customer service industry—for example, retail, food service, or a call center. However, if you're searching for a professional job you still may want to give it a try.

TIP #1:

PICK THE RIGHT TIME

Imagine a restaurant during the lunch or dinner rush. The waiters are all waiting on five tables each, and it takes ten minutes for the hostess to notice you're standing at the front door in your best shoes. Now imagine that the manager is at least twice as busy as the hostess. Are you picturing this? Good. Now you know why you should have applied for a restaurant job in the afternoon, sometime between the lunch rush and the dinner rush.

For retail positions, timing is slightly less important, but you'll still want to avoid angering testy managers. If you go to apply for a job and there's a line out the door waiting to check out, or return things, or complain, come back later.

TIP #2:

BE PREPARED

Although you're going to have a fantastic résumé after you read our résumé chapter, many businesses will ask you to fill out their silly little application anyway. Never ask for a pen. Bring one of your own. Also, bring all the information you'll need in order to fill out the application— employment history, addresses and phone numbers of previous employers, phone numbers of references, and your Social Security number, of course.

Bring your own pen

TIP #3:

DON'T ASK THE RECEPTIONIST/CASHIER/HOST/HOSTESS FOR A JOB

He or she cannot hire you. On the other hand, don't be rude—the first person you see when you walk into a restaurant or shop probably won't be the manager, but he or she will probably talk about you to the manager as soon as you're gone. Politely ask to see a manager. Avoid the temptation to ask for an application and then run. Introduce yourself, and then move on to Tip #4.

TIP #4:

ASK QUESTIONS

Find out the name of the manager you're speaking to. If the manager's not available, you might try talking to an employee if he or she appears willing to chat (don't be pushy). Whomever you speak with, ask what kind of positions are open, and try to get some details, like how many hours a week you'd be working, and what the busiest shifts are. You'll want to know this information in case you're offered a job. Also, asking the

Don't ask the sales clerk for a job

questions will give you a chance to show off your good conversational skills and professional demeanor. If you're saying, "What good conversational skills and professional demeanor?" check out Interviewing on Page 41.

TIP #5:

DRESS THE PART

You should try to dress like the people who have the job you want. For more tips on wardrobe, see Dress Cool on Page 44.

TIP #6:

QUANTITY IS QUALITY

If all this is starting to sound like an unlikely way to land a job, that's because it is. The best way to make beating the streets work is to apply to as many places as you can. Don't be picky now. If you get tons of job offers, then you can be picky.

GET DOWN AND DIRTY: ALL ABOUT NETWORKING

Frankly, if all you do is hit the streets or search the want ads, you're going to have trouble finding a professional job—or at least a professional job you really want. And even if you're looking for part-time work in the service industry, using the number one most effective job hunting skill—networking—is likely to help you land a job faster, or at a place where you'll enjoy working more.

So what is networking? Basically, it's a fancy word for using all the connections you have with people you know in order to get a leg in the door. Most career counselors agree that networking is hands down the best way to find a job. There are two good ways to make networking work:

1.
Use your existing connections.
Surely someone you know is employed and has an inside connection to a job you'd like to be considered for. Ask for favors! Does your girlfriend's dad own a video production company, and you've always wanted to be a video editor? Ask if he has any available positions, or if he knows anyone in the industry who's hiring. Is your long-lost best friend from high school now the president of a diamond importing conglomerate? Perhaps she's hiring administrative assistants. The

key here is to be polite, but shameless—you need a job, and you shouldn't be afraid to ask for one. Your friends and family understand the position you're in—they've been there themselves. You're not a mooch just for asking around. (You are a mooch, however, if you're conveniently "in the neighborhood" around dinner time and you plop yourself down asking, "What's cooking?" as you chug the last of someone's orange juice straight from the jug. For Pete's sake, get a life.)

2.
Make new connections.
After you've exhausted and/or alienated your closest friends, relatives, and even distant acquaintances and still haven't found a job, you can take networking to the next level. How? By networking with people you don't even know! This is easier than it sounds. Just follow these simple steps.

■ Figure out a few places you'd like to work, do some research about who's in charge of the department you're most interested in, and then write to them, expressing your interest in learning about what they do.

■ Follow up within a week or so and try to schedule an appointment, just to ask for some advice. The idea is to get yourself seated across from someone in a position of power in your chosen field.

■ Once there, you can ask questions about the industry, including such important questions as, "How does one go about getting involved in your business?" and

"Do you have any recommendations for someone who's interested in working in your field?"

■ Treat this as an "informational interview" and don't ask for a job point blank—you don't want this guy thinking you brought him here on false pretenses. The point is to cultivate a connection that may be helpful to you one way or another.

MORE NETWORKING TIPS

Whether you're networking with people you know or complete strangers, one good way to avoid seeming pushy is to ask, "Is there anyone else I could get in touch with to talk about working in this field?" That way you're not asking for a job—you're just making your interest in a job clear. If the person you're talking to has a job for you, she'll say, "Yes, you should talk to me." If she doesn't have anything for you, she might give you a few names to help build your network of contacts. Hey—maybe that's why they call it networking.

ONLINE JOB SEARCH SITES: DO THEY WORK?

Visiting online job search companies like Monster.com, Hotjobs.com, and Careerpath.com can be an excellent way to find employment opportunities—and in fact it's the only way to find jobs with some employers who have abandoned traditional advertisements, preferring the ease and speed of the Internet.

These sites also make the legwork easier because they allow you to apply online by forwarding your cover letter and résumé to prospective employers. And they let you run targeted searches for the specific kinds of jobs you want (and that are likely to want you), so it can be more efficient than searching through pages and pages of print ads.

Lastly, the Internet is a global resource, which means you may get responses from companies or places you never would have imagined. It can literally open up a whole world of opportunities.

However, here are a few things to keep in mind if you decide to use the Internet in your job search.

18

1. Make sure you use the proper format for your résumé. Some job sites have online forms or wizards you can use when creating your résumé. If the site's wizard doesn't allow you to spell check, however, try creating your résumé off-line, using a plain text format, and then importing it into the site. That way, you can ensure that you haven't accidentally typed "strange" when you meant to type "strong."

great place to find a job!

2. Privacy can be an issue on some web sites, so make sure you use a well-known, reputable posting service. You don't want your personal information just floating out there for anyone to access. Some sites use the fine print to inform you that once you post, your résumé becomes the property of the site. They can then sell your information to other search companies or use it as part of a résumé blasting campaign.

3. Post your résumé with a few select services rather than hitting all of them. You want to avoid over exposing yourself, so have a plan. If your résumé pops up a zillion times in a recruiter's search, you run the risk of being labeled a résumé spammer, which won't make you popular.

4. Be patient and persistent. It's not unusual to have your résumé forwarded for 100 advertised positions and receive only 5 nibbles. On the other hand, if your résumé hasn't generated a response in a month, consider retooling it or moving it to another site.

5. Internet posting should be one of many job search tactics. The same advice applies here as elsewhere in this guide: posting your résumé and hoping someone stumbles across it like pirate's gold is lousy job hunting. Use multiple approaches!

19

HEADHUNTERS

Picture a tropical island with lots of decapitated heads on pikes. Now stop picturing it, because that's not what we mean when we say headhunters. A headhunter is someone who helps people find jobs and helps businesses find employees—kind of a matchmaker for the business world. Headhunters are also referred to as "employment agencies" and "search firms." If a headhunter works solo, he or she can be called a "recruiter" or "search consultant."

Headhunters are indispensable at the highest levels of business, but even if you don't yet have a parking space with your name on it, a headhunter may be able to help you out. Here's how it works:

1.
Find a headhunter who specializes in your area of interest. Most recruiters focus on a specific industry, so if you're interested in international education, you might steer clear of Edna's Engineering Employment. You should also ask any prospective headhunter for references to make sure they're reputable.

2.
Your headhunter now interviews you, then tries to match you with an employer.

3.
Headhunters are usually paid by the companies that retain them (your future employers, you hope), although some may charge you a fee as well. Be wary if they ask you for money. Frankly, you shouldn't have to pay to get a job. Free recruiting options can be found through your school job placement service, guidance counselors, and job fairs.

4.
Headhunters do not have to agree to help you with your job hunt. They won't try to find you a job if they don't think you're qualified, because that would ruin their credibility with the companies for whom they recruit. That's why asking a headhunter to take you on is sort of like interviewing for a job. Be prepared—see Interviewing on Page 41.

5.
Headhunters can also help you polish your interviewing and résumé writing skills.

Not that kind of headhunter!

TEMPORARY EMPLOYMENT AGENCIES

Temporary employment is exactly what it sounds like: you sign up with a temp agency, and they land you jobs that can last anywhere from a day to a few months. The obvious benefit of this is that you can do temp work to pay the bills while looking for a permanent job. The less obvious but equally important benefit is that every time you work a temp job, you're adding to your list of networking contacts. Some temporary positions are "temp-to-hire," meaning that if they like you, they might take you on full-time. But even the purely temporary jobs allow you to meet and impress people who might hire you later, or who might know someone else who will hire you later. At the very least, you want to make a good impression so that the temp agency keeps sending you out for other jobs.

Temp agencies, like recruiters, often specialize in one industry or another. Much of the work is clerical or secretarial, but some agencies specialize in labor, like construction.

Generally, the more specialized temp agencies will be able to offer you work more often, because they draw from a smaller pool of more specialized workers. If you're good at typing, filing, making coffee, answering phones, and translating written and spoken Mandarin and Cantonese, you could sign up with a temp agency that specializes in placing administrative assistants, but you'd be better off with an agency that specializes in international business or translation. Use your skills, especially the skills no one else has.

Also, there's no rule that says you can't sign up at more than one temp agency at a time. Do not, however, sign up at seven different temp agencies. You'll end up turning down offers left and right, and unlike your friends, who are easily impressed by your apparent popularity, temp agencies just find this annoying.

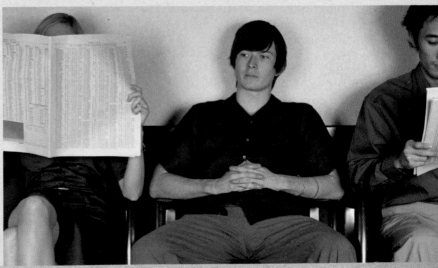

21

HUNTING FOR INTERNSHIPS

I nternships have a lot to recommend them— especially if you're still in school or a recent graduate. Essentially, an internship is a 3 to 12 month job with a company, full or part time, paid or unpaid. You can even get high school or college credit for your work.

Sounds glamorous, huh? Well, the glam factor is hit or miss for interns. Some internships in fields like journalism or television will have you out on the beat filing real stories and getting excellent work experience. Other internships—even in the same industry—will have you out on the beat fetching lattes and couriering packages. And we've all seen what David Letterman does with his interns. (Can anyone spell humiliation?)

But the balance is more good than bad, especially when you consider that good internships offer experiences you would never get in an entry-level job, where you really will be expected to do a lot of typing and coffee making. And the best news is that if you're very good, you might be offered a full-time position at the end of your internship.

INTERNSHIP HUNTING TIPS

1 The easiest way to find internship possibilities is to go to your college career placement office. However, this becomes less easy if you don't happen to be in college. In that case, check out one of the many annually published research guides that list every internship known to man. Visit www.realuguides.com for links.

2 Start early. If you want a position for the summer after you graduate, don't wait until May to get started looking. Internship hunting is something of an extreme sport, and so for the best jobs, you may have to start applying as much as nine months in advance.

3 Practice good networking skills. Get names and contact info from everyone you work for or with at your internship. (That way, if they suck you dry and then spit you out without a job offer at the end of your internship, at least you'll know where these guys live.)

4 Have a good résumé and cover letter ready, and practice your interviewing skills. Although companies know you're a student, they still expect you to have your act together. Good luck!

JOB HUNTING FOR
RECENT COLLEGE GRADS

Sometime during your sophomore year at college, perhaps midway through your Ancient Etruscan Burial Rights midterm, you probably began to wonder why exactly you were spending four years studying things like, well, say, Ancient Etruscan Burial Rights. Although for a few days after that you probably skipped class and despaired for your future and that of your unborn children, you eventually settled down with the thought that once you had a college degree, finding a job would be a whole lot easier.

Yeah, and it would have been, if you hadn't majored in Ancient Etruscan Burial Rights, you big idiot.

Some college majors lead pretty directly to a profession. Practical majors like engineering, education, and architecture, for instance, certainly put you on some kind of career path.

But say you've spent four (or five, or six) years getting your degree in elementary education and you decide that, oops, you hate kids. What then? Or what if you really did major in sociology, in spite of your parents' constant pleas that you study air conditioning repair? Here are a few tips to help you avoid what we like to call PCSS, or Post-Collegiate Stress Syndrome.

What exactly were you going to do with your major in Ancient Etruscan Burial Rights?

Don't worry about finding the perfect job straight out of college.

1 Be open to possibilities. Don't be discouraged when people ask you what you're going to do with your degree, especially if your degree is in the humanities, pure sciences, or the arts. Your attitude should be: What can't I do?

2 Don't worry about your relatively empty résumé. No one expects recent grads to have tons of job experience—you've been in school for the past four years. For now, your education will go at the top of your résumé, and you'll fill in job experience later. (For more on résumé writing, go to Page 27.)

3 Unless you want to work in academia, think about taking some time off before going to grad school. Yeah, it can be tempting to opt out of the rat race by going back to college, but trust us: grad student parties aren't nearly as good as the undergrad ones, and you don't want to be the creepy 23-year-old who keeps showing up at freshman keggers.

4 Don't worry about finding the perfect job straight out of college. Even if you have a good sense of what kind of work you want to do, you'll probably still have to take an entry-level position—possibly one for which you're overqualified—and work your way up to your dream job. In most industries it's called "paying your dues."

5 In some industries, however, these entry level positions are called "working a dead-end job." Some businesses—and even some entire industries—are notorious for hiring recent grads to do the grunt work and then, just when the person would normally expect a promotion or raise, they fire the guy and hire someone just as innocent to take his place. Use your networking skills to find out in advance if your big first job offer is a big waste of time. However, even if you find out that you are being used like a disposable ballpoint pen, you may still want to take the job because of Tip Number 6.

6 Whether you're offered a dead-end job in your industry or a good job in a field where you don't want to work, taking the offer may still be better than not. Why? Because it's easier to hunt for a job when you're currently employed. If prospective employers see that you've got a job, they know you're not a total loser. And prospective employers like that sort of thing.

HOW TO WRITE A GREAT RÉSUMÉ

> If you had your druthers, your résumé would be dozens of pages long, leaving you plenty of room for footnotes explaining why you were a few credits short of finishing that Masters degree, or why your previous boss might still froth at the mouth at the mention of your name.

Unfortunately, your entire résumé is supposed to fit on a single sheet of 8½ by 11 inch bond. Because résumés are so brief, you'll want to pick your words carefully in order to put just the right spin on your skills and experience. Don't sweat it if some details get left out. Keep in mind that the point of a résumé isn't to get you a job—it's to get you an interview for a job. Your résumé should be designed to pique a would-be employer's interest. You can fill in the nuances of your summer goat herding internship later, at the interview.

Use different résumés for different jobs

YOUR RÉSUMÉ QUESTIONS – ANSWERED!

What jobs require a résumé?

Nearly all of them. It used to be that résumés were only required for professional positions, but since the standards for employees are rising with every passing day, it can't hurt to include a résumé with any job application. At the very least, it shows your prospective employer that you have your act together.

Should I put my GPA on my résumé?

Only if it's a 3.0 or higher. Frankly, your experience and the way you present it is more important, especially if your grades were only so-so.

Résumé services: Are they worth it?

Not usually. These services charge a fee, and often they simply use the same formats and templates you can get on your computer, from a web site, or from this book. You could end up paying a lot for something you could have done better yourself. Try to find free resources like school job services and professional friends or family members. Ideally, look for someone who hires people himself and looks at a lot of résumés in the process. If you need advanced résumé tips, go to the library and find a few of the gazillion or so books on résumé writing. Many have self-assessments to help you develop your résumé.

Should I have different versions of my résumé for different jobs?

Definitely. If you're applying for jobs in several different fields—or even different positions within the same field—you'll want to tailor your résumé to the specific job. Find out as much as you can about the job you're applying for, and choose the experiences and skills that are most relevant. Acme Tire Supply probably won't care that you bussed tables part time in high school, but George's Steakhouse will.

Honesty on your résumé: How important is it?

Very. Padding your résumé can get you into big trouble. Obviously, you shouldn't tell a whopper—for instance that you attended medical school when you didn't—unless you want to go to prison. But even little white lies, like jobs you didn't have or classes you didn't take, can get you into trouble. If you're caught, you'll most likely be fired and it will definitely ruin your chances for a favorable recommendation. Having said that, understand that modesty has no place on a résumé. You can and should talk up your real skills and talents. Be proud of yourself and your accomplishments.

> EVEN LITTLE WHITE LIES, LIKE JOBS YOU DIDN'T HAVE OR CLASSES YOU DIDN'T TAKE, CAN GET YOU INTO TROUBLE.

More résumé tips ⟶

Here's a step-by-step guide to writing a résumé that will put the best possible spin on the life you've led so far.

Brainstorming...

1.

BRAINSTORMING YOUR LIFE EXPERIENCE

Before you start writing your résumé, you need to spend some time thinking about what you're going to put on it. Grab a sheet of paper and make some lists. This is a brainstorm, so write down everything you can think of, even if you think it's not worth putting on your résumé. Here are the main areas you should hit:

Writing

Education:

For most first time résumé writers, academic experience is often the most relevant information. (For some, it's your only experience.) List your school, the highest degree you attained, and the year you graduated. If you haven't finished school, use the dates you attended school instead of the degree. If you have attended more than one college, tech school, or university, list them all starting with the one you attended most recently. Include all post-graduate work as well. List all coursework related to the field you're trying to enter, especially if you're applying in a field that's clearly outside your major. Remember: this is just the brainstorming list. You may not put this stuff on your résumé, but it doesn't hurt to consider it.

Experiences, Activities, and Projects:

Write down every job or internship you've had since you were born. You can include leadership positions you held in college—newspaper editor, volunteer EMS worker, president of the Young Socialists League, etc.—especially if these jobs are relevant to the kind of work you're looking for. Keep in mind that anything at all can count as experience, whether or not it was a "real" job. Think broadly. Even if you weren't paid for doing something before, you can still use it as a reason why you should be paid now. If you helped organize a rummage sale at your church, that's great. Any kind of leadership position you've held is likely to impress an employer, even if it's not in the same field as the job. It proves you take initiative, and that's good in any job.

Awards and Honors:

If you've ever won anything or been recognized for exceptionally good work, write it down. If you have not, do not put the heading, "Awards and Honors," followed by a blank space. That's just depressing.

Special Skills:

Most companies don't really care that you can juggle chainsaws. List computer skills (including what software applications and operating systems you're comfortable with), languages you speak or write, industry-specific knowledge you've acquired, and so forth. Competitive sports teams are good, too. They show you have discipline and can work well with other people. If you have room at the bottom, go ahead and list the chainsaws. Maybe the boss is into it, too!

2.
PICKING AND CHOOSING

Now it's time to choose which items make the cut. Take the list you made and circle the items that are directly related to the job you're applying for. Those will make it for sure.

Next, circle any experiences or skills that are particularly impressive, even if they're not clearly relevant. No matter what job you're applying for, an employer will want to know if you are a master chess player, or if you know how to restore old motorcycles, or if *Woodwind Quarterly* named you the hottest young bassoon player in the upper Midwest.

Finally, think broadly. What other experiences will show you off well? The fact that you worked in your mom's coffee shop in high school doesn't exactly qualify you to work at an air conditioning repair company all by itself, but it still shows that you can report to work on time, handle being on your feet for long periods, and deal with customers. If it looks like you're going to have space, adding these items can only help you.

3.
LAYING OUT YOUR RÉSUMÉ

You should now have a list of everything about you that makes you an attractive candidate for the job. And really, that's all a résumé is—a long list of your credentials. But because a single list with many entries is hard to interpret, an effective résumé breaks the list up into small, manageable sections that organize your qualifications in a clear, logical form.

A one-page résumé should have 3 or 4 sections, each with 2-4 entries in them. Within each section, list your most recent experiences first. If you're listing something like a skill, which doesn't have a specific date, just put whatever is most impressive first. Your first section will probably be "Education." You know what goes there.

The second section should group together your most clearly relevant work and volunteer experiences. Instead of just titling it "Work Experience," though, you

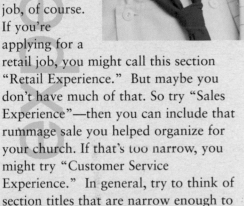

want a title that describes specifically what the items have in common. This depends on the job, of course. If you're applying for a retail job, you might call this section "Retail Experience." But maybe you don't have much of that. So try "Sales Experience"—then you can include that rummage sale you helped organize for your church. If that's too narrow, you might try "Customer Service Experience." In general, try to think of section titles that are narrow enough to seem especially relevant to the job you're applying for, but broad enough to

encompass all the different experiences you've actually had. More suggestions:

- "Administrative Experience"
- "Business Experience"
- "Research Experience"
- "Leadership Experience"
- "Writing Experience"
- "Communications Experience"

You get the idea. If you really can't think of the right title for this section, you can always just use "Experience," but the more specific you can be, the better.

Subsequent sections of your résumé will list the things that are less clearly related to the job you're applying for but still worth including. Consider the following possible titles:

ADDITIONAL EXPERIENCE

VOLUNTEER EXPERIENCE

SKILLS

AWARDS & HONORS

OTHER INTERESTS

4.
GET DOWN WITH THE LINGO

Now, for each entry include a short description of your most important responsibilities and whatever skills you obtained. It's fine to use bullet points and sentence fragments. A line or two for each entry is usually fine. Use powerful verbs with punch to describe your activities. Some good ones: led, managed, organized, created, built, developed, assisted, designed, prepared, contributed, transformed, researched, instigated, spearheaded, masterminded...O.K., maybe not those last three.

5.
PROOFREAD AND TWEAK

You may have all the credentials in the world, but if your résumé has misspellings, grammatical errors, and typos, it tells an employer that either you're careless and sloppy, or that you just don't respect him enough to do your best work. Neither impression will further your job prospects. So ask a friend or family member to look over your résumé before you finalize it. Finally, print a copy and take a look at the whole thing: Does it fit on one page? Is it crisp and easy to read? Are the spacing and fonts consistent throughout? Did you remember to put your address, phone number, fax (if you have one), and e-mail at the top by your name? Make the final tweaks. This is like that last check-up in the mirror before a date. You check your hair, straighten your tie, or touch up your makeup. Your résumé is your first impression, and you only get one chance.

6.
PRINT IT

Be a grown-up. Use professional-looking stationery in heavy bond. This means no rainbow novelty paper, metallic, or laser cutouts. The exception to this rule is if you are applying for a position in a truly creative industry, like design or theater. Even then, be careful.

To see more examples of typical resumes, visit

www.realuguides.com

34

E R I N   M c S A M P L E

123 Sample Street No. 4
Rhinebeck, NY 12505
(914) 555-1234
e-mc-s@sampleton.net

you might want a summary

don't forget your contact info!

SUMMARY

I am a recent graduate with a Masters degree and two years of writing and editorial experience. I am looking for an editorial position which will allow me to use the detail-oriented, deadline-driven leadership skills I developed as an editor and writer.

EDUCATION

recent grads – put education first

2002-2004	State University of New York, Binghamton • MA in Ancient Etruscan Art • Graduated magna cum laude	Binghamton, NY
1998-2002	New Jersey Community College • BA in Anthropology	Paterson, NJ

EDITORIAL/LEADERSHIP EXPERIENCE

most recent experience first

2003-2004	**Associate Editor**, Etruscan Burial Quarterly • Edited and produced a quarterly journal on Etruscan burial rites • Led a team of 3 editorial assistants and proofreaders in deadline-oriented production	Binghamton, NY
1998-2000	**Member**, NJ Community College Debate Team • Voted Most Valuable Debater, 2000	Paterson, NJ

OTHER WORK EXPERIENCE

Summer 1997	**Sales Associate**, Paula's Pet Paradise	Newark, NJ
Summer 1998	**Sales Associate**, Franz's Floral Fantasy	Paramus, NJ

SKILLS AND QUALIFICATIONS

Computer skills:
Microsoft Office Suite
General computer proficiency on Mac and PC

Other skills:
Juggling chainsaws

HOW TO WRITE A GREAT COVER LETTER

What is a cover letter anyway?

Essentially, a cover letter is a brief introduction that persuasively highlights the reasons why you should be honored with an interview. A cover letter is not always required, but it's always a good idea. Most professional positions will ask for one, especially in careers for which verbal and written skills are necessary. If you're responding to an advertised position, you may be asked to answer some specific questions in your cover letter. Take these seriously, even if they seem stupid.

A cover letter is also a chance to show a bit of your personality. Your qualifications are the most important element, but your potential employer also knows he may be spending a large portion of his life working with you. As with your résumé, your cover letter may be the employer's zillionth of the day. So liven it up. A joke or personal anecdote can endear you to the reader as long as it's in good taste.

10

TOP TO BOTTOM TIPS TO A PERFECT COVER LETTER

1.

This is a business letter, so use appropriate stationery—no bizarre colors or prints. Keep it classic. Better yet, print it on the same paper as your résumé. Your cover letter should be typed in block business format with your return address above the date. And forget about cutesy fonts—use a 12-point book quality type.

2.

Don't begin you letter "Dear Sir or Madam" if at all possible, especially if you are inquiring for an informational interview. Do some investigating and find out exactly to whom your letter should be addressed. This is sometimes more difficult if you are applying for an advertised position, but try anyway.

3.

In your first paragraph, say why you're writing—explain the purpose of the letter. If you're writing in response to an advertisement or at the suggestion of a mutual friend, say so.

4.

Mention that you have enclosed your résumé for their reference, and then move right on to highlighting some of your accomplishments. Whatever you do, don't simply repeat what's on your résumé. It's boring and redundant. A cover letter is your chance to be specific about where your qualifications intersect with the needs of the employer, so explain why you were made employee of the month.

5.

Use the active voice and strong verbs—it communicates your enthusiasm and strength.

6.

Show you know something about the organization where you want to work. Do some research and be specific. If it's a carpet company, tell them you admire their patented stain-proof coating. If it's a restaurant, tell them you adore the grilled salmon. But don't just praise. Explain how your knowledge of their operation makes you that much more excited to be a part of the team and more confident that you're qualified.

7.

If you're applying for a specific position, wrap it up by reiterating how interested you are in the job. For an informational interview, mention how interested you are in learning about the business. List the hours and phone number at which you can be reached.

8.

Use a professional closing such as "Sincerely" or "Yours truly," and sign your name above your typed name.

9.

To err is human, to proofread, divine. It is imperative that your cover letter be completely free of mistakes—no misspellings, typos, or grammatical errors.

10.

For advertised positions, follow up within a week by phone or e-mail. Ask whether there's any additional information you could provide, and offer some references. Keep it brief.

APPLYING & INTERVIEWING

Congratulations!

All that hard work you put into your job hunt, résumé, and cover letter has finally paid off. Well, almost. The interview is the biggest hurdle between you and employment, so get psyched. This is your big chance to woo your prospective employer, and wow them with your competence and congeniality!

That said, remember that an interview is a two-way street. They aren't just grilling you—you're interviewing them as well. An interview is kind of like a first date. It's a conversation during which you and your prospective employer will try to see how you'll mesh. In fact, some companies like to "date" candidates for a while before making a decision. It's not unusual to have several interviews (like, five) before a proposal is made...if at all.

HOW TO PREPARE FOR AN
INTERVIEW

Remember your targeted résumé and cover letter? And how you explained that your qualifications would serve the company and vice versa? Well, you're going to do it all again...in person. It's time to strut your stuff. Here's what you do:

■ Know the industry—more importantly, know the company you're interviewing with. The worst

thing you can do is to walk into the interview and start babbling about how much you love your Playstation, if the company makes Gamecubes. (Believe it or not, this happens all the time.) Besides protecting you from stupid statements, being an "expert" about the company allows you to assess how well you truly fit.

■ Do some thinking beforehand about the ways in which you really are qualified for the job. Sometimes the process of filling out applications and résumés can get you so focused on convincing others you're qualified that you forget to convince yourself. It's great to appear confident, but it's much better to *be* confident. Learn as much as you can about the actual day-to-day duties of the job you're applying for, and be prepared with concrete examples of tasks you've done in the past that are similar to those you'll be asked to do at your new job.

■ Be prepared also to show off your personal experience with whatever product or service the company sells. For example, if you're applying to be a waitress, tell the manager you ate at the restaurant last week and how impressed you were that the waiter had asked the chef to make chicken fingers especially for your bratty little cousin. That shows you know what good service is.

■ If you're applying at a major corporation, dig up a copy of its annual report or marketing brochures. Search the Internet for any information about the company's business practices, corporate culture, and structure.

■ In general, decide what points you want to emphasize before the interview, and find a way to work them in. Of course, you have to answer the questions you're asked, but it's usually possible to steer a vague question in a direction you want. Don't miss the opportunity to talk about a subject on which you're an expert, or relate an experience that's impressive, just because the interviewer doesn't ask about it directly.

DRESS COOL:

WHAT TO WEAR TO YOUR JOB INTERVIEW

This depends on the work environment. The typical office environment today is less formal than it once was, but particular industries—especially those involving client service—still require business suits. When in doubt, dress up. No one will fault you for it.

Here's a chart about what to wear for various kinds of interviews:

OTHER TIPS:

- [ ] Grooming matters. Get a haircut. Shave and trim as necessary to look respectable. This sort of thing may not matter to your friends, but older people still tend to like a clean look.

- [ ] Don't forget your deodorant. Seriously. You'll be sweating and you don't want to stink. Beware excessive perfume and cologne. Breath mints are a blessing.

- [ ] Don't wear anything so eye-catching—a brightly patterned scarf, tie, or sweater, for example—that it will take the focus away from you. The exception is if you're applying to work in an industry (art, hospitality) where personal style is an important occupational trait.

Retail   Executive   Labor

	Men	Women
Executive Job	Suit and tie	Suit
Office/Administrative Job	Dress shirt, tie, nice slacks, blazer	Skirt and blouse or sweater
Retail/Food Service	Dress shirt, no tie, nice slacks or khakis, blazer optional	Blouse or sweater-top and pants or skirt
Hospitality	Suit and tie	Suit or dressy skirt and blouse
Labor	Jeans or appropriate work clothes, and bring your own tools	Jeans or appropriate work clothes, and bring your own tools
Pop Star	Designer jeans, vintage T-shirt, and bring your own groupies	Low-rise jeans, sparkly halter top, and bring your own lip gloss

TALK THE TALK:
INTERVIEW QUESTIONS AND HOW TO RESPOND

The biggest job hunting mistake you can make is to walk into your job interview wondering what on earth you're going to be asked.

Don't wonder. Figure it out in advance, or better yet, read on and we'll tell you! Then have your answers not only ready—have them memorized, rehearsed, and so polished that you can rattle them off in your sleep. (Hopefully, you won't need to use this level of preparation because you won't be asleep during the interview. If you are, try not to snore.)

When it comes to the classic interview questions, here are a few interviewer favorites:

1. "So, tell me about yourself."

How ironic: the most terrifying interview question in the world isn't even a question. Fight your instinct to babble (or flee), since this really isn't difficult to answer. The interviewer is just trying to find out where you're coming from and whether or not you have any idea about where you're going. A two or three minute answer is usually long enough. Lead off with a positive personality trait that relates to your choice of employment, for example, "I like dealing with people, so I thought I would succeed in retail." Then spend a few minutes explaining how you became interested in the industry and what you've done to prepare for a position. Be modest but confident. Also, understand that anything you bring up here is fair game for future questions, so know what you're talking about. End with a short, interesting fact about yourself that gives the interviewer a glimpse at something about you that might be memorable, that might set you apart from every other applicant. If possible, try to tie it in to the job qualifications.

Examples:

"I come from a family of 8, so I'm used to dealing with a lot of chaos at mealtimes."

"I love to problem solve—as a hobby, I debug computer programs for my friends."

"I'm a high energy person—on weekends, I compete in amateur mountain bike events."

Problem solver

2. "What are your strengths?"

Well, what are they? Are you a good listener? A good talker? Are you supremely organized? Be decisive about your strengths—pick one or two that most accurately represent you (and relate to the job you want)—and briefly elaborate on them. (E.g. "I'm willing to take charge. As treasurer of my church youth group, it was my job to plan bake sales and an auction to raise money for our mission trip to Guatemala.")

3. "What's your biggest weakness?"

If possible, this question sucks more than question number one. The trick to answering this is to use the least amount of negative language you can. Mention your weakness briefly, and then explain how you've been proactive about changing, eliminating, or compensating for it. Don't say, "I'm disorganized." Instead, say something like, "I've struggled a bit with organization. But I've taken charge of that by developing a well thought-out filing system and consulting my day planner religiously." Another trick is to choose a weakness that's usually a strength. For example, "Sometimes I'm too detail-oriented. I put a lot of effort into small tasks, even when it would be better to finish up quickly and move on." But don't be too blatant about it: saying you're a perfectionist will earn you an eye roll. Sincerity will get you props, so stick with the truth. You're probably not as good a liar as you think you are.

Note: Companies are not allowed to ask you any questions about your age, race, religion, sexual identity, marital status, or plans for parenthood. If you are asked one of these questions, try to deflect it and change the subject. If the interviewer persists, say something like, "I don't see how that relates to the position." End the interview if the questions become too personal or inappropriate.

High energy

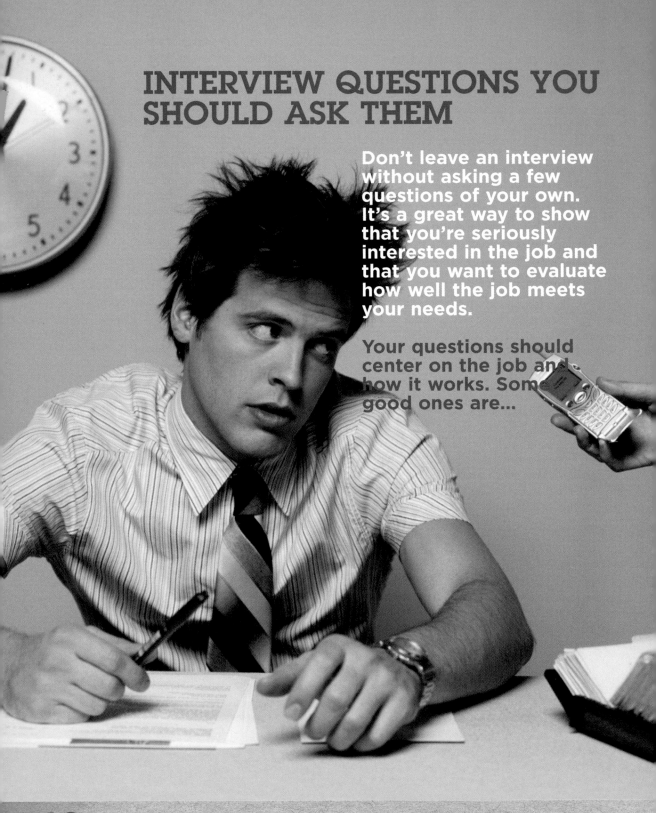

INTERVIEW QUESTIONS YOU SHOULD ASK THEM

Don't leave an interview without asking a few questions of your own. It's a great way to show that you're seriously interested in the job and that you want to evaluate how well the job meets your needs.

Your questions should center on the job and how it works. Some good ones are...

1. What would a typical day look like?

 2. What kind of positions does this job lead to? Is there room for advancement?

3. Tell me about the corporate environment here? What do you like about this company?

If you can work in some of the information you uncovered during your research, do so. If you're interviewing for a corporate job, you don't want to ask how much money you'll make. It's cheeky and tacky. Let them bring up the dollars first. (Then hope they bring up a few more!) If you're applying for a job that pays by the hour, however, you should feel free to ask what the wages are before the interview is over.

GETTING REFERENCES

One of the last steps in the interview process is checking your references. A prospective employer will expect you to be prepared with the names, titles, phone numbers, and addresses for three to five people who know you well. You want people who are informed and impressed by your skills and can speak intelligently about them. Teachers, former employers, supervisors, counselors, ministers, coaches, and activity leaders are good choices.

When gathering your references make sure to ask the people if it's O.K. to list them as a reference. If they say no, cross them off your list. It's also helpful to let your references know what position you are applying for. That way they won't be caught off guard and can respond to any specific questions that might relate to the job. Better yet, send them a copy of your résumé.

FOLLOWING UP: HOW, WHEN, AND HOW OFTEN

So the interview is over. Whew. But don't slack off now.

If you really want the job, you've got to follow up. Your first step is to send your interviewer a typed thank you letter immediately after your meeting. This demonstrates your good manners and keeps your interview fresh in her mind.

Start the letter by thanking the interviewer for her time and then mention how much you enjoyed the interview or meeting. Go on to briefly remind her how your skills mesh with the requirements of the job, using something that came up during your discussion as an example. Close by thanking her again for her consideration and let her know that you are available to answer any other questions.

Sometimes the hiring process takes forever, so don't freak out if you haven't heard anything within a week or two. If several weeks have passed, and you still haven't heard anything, go ahead and follow up with a phone call to see if the position has been filled. If it has, thank the person for his or her time. If it hasn't, use the opportunity to remind him/her of your qualifications.

CONGRATULATIONS!

YOU GOT THE JOB!

There are few things better than getting the "you're hired" phone call. When it comes, take a moment to pat yourself on the back. After all, you worked hard to get here.

Depending on what kind of job you've just landed, you may be able to take a few days to think about whether you even want to accept it, or you might have to give them an answer right away.

If it's a job waiting tables at the hottest new restaurant in town, and you've never been a server before, thank your lucky stars that they've given you a shot at it and say yes. Ditto for any job in a tight market where you know there's been a lot of competition. On the other hand, if you're not sure this job is right for you, you have every reason to take a little time to think it over. Either way, you should calmly express your pleasure about being offered the position. And then, before you accept any job, you'll need to know three key things:

1. Wages and salary

2. Benefits

3. Advancement policy

As always, it's a good idea to do some research and be prepared to discuss these issues with your new employer. Lucky for you, we've done some of that research for you. Read on!

MONEY MONEY MONEY

Ideally, you should find out what a fair wage or salary is for the job you're interested in before you slide into the first interview. It can be tricky to figure this out, but it's worth the effort to try to determine a good salary for the position and region.

If the job advertisement didn't specify a salary range, ask friends in the biz, check out the government's Occupational Outlook Handbook, or surf the web. However you do it, be prepared to discuss the offer by knowing your dream salary as well as your bottom line. Some jobs have a specific "pay  grade" attached, which means your employer can't offer you any more than the amount in the guidelines. But other salaries are negotiable. Stick to your guns, but be polite and realistic when negotiating. They aren't going to offer you $30 an hour to flip burgers, no matter how much you play hardball. Also, don't forget about the other things the company is offering you, like benefits.

Here's a chart of the typical salary ranges for various kinds of jobs →

SALARY RANGES

JOB	SALARY (IN THOUSANDS)
	0 10 20 30 40 50 60 70 80 90 100 110 120 130 140 150
Accountant	approx. 35–85
Administrative Assistant	approx. 20–50
Airline Pilot	approx. 60–150
Architect	approx. 35–95
Bank Teller	approx. 20–30
Chemical Engineer	approx. 50–105
Computer Programmer	approx. 45–95
Construction Laborer	approx. 20–50
Cook/Chef	approx. 20–85
Electrician	approx. 35–60
High School Teacher	approx. 35–65
Hotel Clerk	approx. 20–45
Lawyer	approx. 55–150
LP Nurse	approx. 35–55
Paralegal	approx. 35–55
Pharmacist	approx. 55–95
Photographer	approx. 45–85
Physician	approx. 40–150
Police Officer	approx. 35–60
Real Estate	approx. 35–140
Sales Clerk, apparel	approx. 20–40
Waiter	approx. 15–75

Not all jobs offer benefits. For those that do, it's a real plus, and you shouldn't underestimate the value of it in your whole compensation package. If, in addition to your salary, the company offers some combination of insurance (health and life), vacation, family leave, and a retirement plan, that's real money. In many cases, it's the equivalent of being paid another $2,000-$10,000 per year.

1. Health Insurance:
Insurance packages usually include some combination of health, dental, vision, and life insurance. The company will often absorb a portion of the cost of your coverage (from 25% to 100%), making it much more affordable for you and your family to stay healthy.

2. Vacation:
A typical vacation plan starts with five days after the first year, and 7–10 days after that. Very few companies in the United States offer more than two to three weeks of vacation annually to start. Make sure to ask about sick days, holidays, and personal days or you could end up having to use up your vacation the next time you get the flu.

3. Family Leave:
The federal government passed the Family and Medical Leave Act in 1993, requiring employers with 50 or more employees to offer up to 12 weeks unpaid leave per year in case of the birth of a child or extended illness of the employee or a close family member. Specific durations and pay status vary by company, so ask.

4. Retirement:
Okay, so you aren't thinking about retirement yet—you just got your first real job! But even if you're barely into your 20's, if your employer offers a retirement plan, you'll want to take advantage of it. The most common kind of retirement plan offered by employers is called a 401(k) plan. It's an investment account that provides you with tax benefits. It usually works like this: you contribute a portion of your paycheck each year, and after you've been employed for a certain period of time, your employer will begin to match your contribution, up to a specified limit. You authorize your employer to deduct a specific amount from your pay each month before taxes are calculated. The money you contribute to your 401(k) (and the money from your employer if you stick around long enough) can move with you from job to job (unlike that wobbly chair you've been using, that's missing a few casters).

MOVING UP

Another important fact to uncover is whether or not the company has room for you to move up the ladder (especially important if you're working in the roofing business). You want to know: Are there higher level positions you can move into? If so, are they filled from within the organization or do they recruit from outside? If your job involves tips, ask about how the most lucrative shifts are assigned. Sure, you may have to start working the slow shifts, but will you get a chance to move into working at peak hours? Or do some old-timers have a lock on them? You didn't go through all this hard work to get stuck in a dead-end job. On the other hand, you can gain valuable experience and contacts working for a year or two, even at a job where you don't have much upward mobility.

Is there room at the top?

HOW (AND WHY) TO TURN DOWN A JOB OFFER

Just because you're offered a job doesn't mean you have to take it. The best-case scenario for turning down a job is if you have another job offer that pays better and/or interests you more. However, even if you've only got one offer, you'll have to decide whether you think a better one will come along soon. You don't want to be locked into a new job just when something better comes along, and in general, you shouldn't plan on quitting a job you've just started unless you've been clear with your employer from the beginning that the job will be temporary. It's a small world, and employers can make you regret jerking them around. Whatever your reasons are for refusing a job offer, make sure you do it politely. Most industries are incredibly incestuous—you can never be sure who knows whom. In addition, just because you don't want to work for X-Corp today doesn't mean you won't be looking for a job with them in few years. Therefore, if you're going to refuse a position, do it in a graciously written letter. Thank the employer for offering to hire you, but don't go into specifics about why you're turning the job down. Simply state that you've decided to go in a different direction.

Now that you've worked so hard to get a job, you need to start thinking about how you're going to hold onto it. Here are ten things you can do to insure your longevity:

1. BE ON TIME.

Occasional tardiness is tolerated, but if you're late more than once a month, your boss will start to think of you as a slacker. Not good.

2. WORK A FULL DAY.

Don't make a practice of cutting out early. Trust us, people will notice.

3. ASK FOR HELP BEFORE THE CRISIS.

If you're confused about what you're supposed to do in any situation, ask for help. Waiting until you've hit crisis mode isn't going to impress anyone.

4. BE PRODUCTIVE.

Do your job and come up with results. That's why they're paying you.

5. PLAY NICE.

Do your best to get along with everyone. One way to stay the nice guy is to not start or spread gossip.

6. HANG WITH THE WINNERS.

Steer clear of the office slacker—however much fun he is. You don't want his label to stick to you.

7. DON'T WHINE.

Unless you have a plan to fix the problem, keep your complaints to yourself.

8. BE OPEN & GRACIOUS TO REQUESTS FOR YOUR HELP.

The words not-in-my-job-description should be not-in-your-vocabulary.

9. BE HONEST.

Try to be truthful yet tactful at all times. Oh, and don't steal office supplies. It's so tacky. Or food, if you work in a restaurant. Or fur coats, if you work at Bloomingdale's.

10. DOCUMENT EVERYTHING.

Develop a filing system where you can keep track of memos sent and received, jobs completed, professional correspondence, everything. You want to be prepared to prove your worth.

HOW TO GET A RAISE IN 3 MONTHS

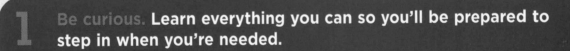

made the deadline!

As you can see from the list on page 56, keeping your job isn't all that difficult. Getting a real raise or a promotion, on the other hand, takes serious focus and dedication. The idea is to make yourself indispensable to your employer. If the company values you, they will give you incentives to keep you happy. Add these skills to your bag of tricks and you'll be rewarded in no time:

1 Be curious. **Learn everything you can so you'll be prepared to step in when you're needed.**

2 Do top-notch work. **A lackluster performance isn't going to impress anybody. Check and recheck your work until it's perfect.**

3 Use your time effectively. **If you finish a project early, don't sit at your desk playing Minesweeper. Ask your boss if there's anything she needs help with.**

4 Meet or beat your deadlines. **Prove that you can get the job done and come through in a pinch.**

5 Be proactive. **If you have a problem, think of ways to solve it before bringing it up to your boss.**

ONWARD & UPWARD: SECOND JOBS AND BEYOND

No matter how much you love your first job,

it's unlikely that you'll work there

until the day you die. And

frankly, not even your boss

expects you to stay where you are forever.

However, when you do go, make sure you do it

with style and class.

Know when it's time to quit!

HOW (AND WHEN) TO QUIT YOUR JOB

There are a number of good reasons to leave your job. You may be promoted within your company, or look for a new challenge elsewhere. Maybe you've stalled at your current position—two or three years is long enough to figure out whether or not you're going anywhere. Perhaps you've realized that you're working at the wrong company or even in the wrong business altogether.

If you're not happy at your present job, it's best to seek a new job while you're still employed. It's always easier to find one that way. Exception: If you're so miserable that you're trashing your boss and co-workers and doing other things that will ultimately sabotage yourself, get out now while your reputation is still intact.

When you know it's time to go, make sure your exit is graceful. Burning bridges can leave you stranded.

A few tips:

1. Inform your immediate boss in person before you tell anyone else. If you work in a large office, follow up with a polite letter of resignation and copy the Human Resources department.

2. Give notice. Two weeks is standard, but if you have complex projects in the works, you might consider staying until they're completed or successfully transferred to someone else.

3. Be positive when anyone asks you why you're leaving, especially in an exit interview. This is not the time to whine and moan about the unfairness of it all. You don't want to be remembered as a complainer.

4. Be open to assisting your successor with the changeover. You might consider offering help via phone or e-mail for a week or two after leaving to insure a smooth transition.

5. On your last day, thank everyone for his or her help and support during your tenure. Remember, your former supervisors and coworkers are now your new networking contacts!

FINDING A NEW JOB

(WHILE YOU'RE STILL AT YOUR OLD ONE)

There are many plusses to looking for a job when you've already got one. It takes the pressure off and shows your prospective employer that it's worth hiring you—after all, someone else has.

If you want to stay in the same industry, keep your ear to the ground for other positions. Talk to people you've worked with from other organizations. Work your contact network for unpublished opportunities. If something comes up that seems intriguing, go ahead and apply, but for goodness sake, be discreet. The worst thing you can do is flaunt your unhappiness at your current job.

Be respectful of your present employer. That means don't use company resources in your job search—no company letterhead, fax machines, copiers, etc. And schedule your interviews on your own time, if at all possible. Remember, until you walk out the door, you still owe your loyalty to the job you have.

GETTING REFERENCES—
AGAIN!

Aha! There *was* a reason you didn't tell your boss to shove it on your last day. Since you'll be adding your former position to your résumé, you'll also want to make sure you get a good reference. As with your other references, you want to make sure your ex-boss is willing to be added to your list. You should also consider asking for a letter of recommendation. An open letter that speaks to your strengths and general qualifications is usually the easiest to take with you. However, if you have an especially strong relationship with your ex-boss, he or she may consider writing you a letter of recommendation specific to each position you apply for. These are the most impressive, but they take extra work on your former employer's part, so be judicious in your request.

NEW JOB: COPING WITH CHANGE

If you were at your last job for a significant time—usually longer than nine months—expect to feel a little homesick and lost. Be confident yet humble. You should assume that your past experience is applicable to your new work environment. After all, that's probably why you got hired. But be prepared to adapt. Don't assume that everything works the same at your new job as it did at your old. Change can be scary. In order to head off any hysteria, go back to the beginning of this book. Looking for your second, or third, or fourth job is not that much different from finding your first. The biggest difference is that you now have more experience and more clout. You're a professional!

Be prepared to adapt!

MORE REAL U...
CHECK OUT THESE OTHER REAL U GUIDES!

YOUR FIRST APARTMENT
Whether you're leaving home for the first time, heading off to college...or skipping the college thing and sliding straight into a real job and real life, this guide has everything you need to know to move out of the house and start your life for real.

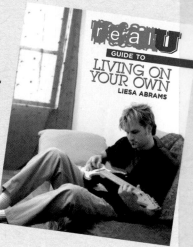

LIVING ON YOUR OWN
So you've finally moved into your first apartment. Now what? Plunge into real life with a safety net. If you can't cook, always shrink your socks, and have no idea where to find your stove's pilot light, this is the guide for you.

BUYING YOUR FIRST CAR
Don't get burned on the first big purchase you make. Find out how to get the best financing, how to avoid the latest scam tactics, whether to buy extended warranties, and more.

FOR MORE INFORMATION ON THESE AND OTHER REAL U GUIDES, VISIT WWW.REALUGUIDES.COM.